BARCELONA ULTIMATE FAN QUIZ

HTplus Editions

Table of Contents

INTRODUCTION...4

GENERAL QUIZ...5

FUN FACTS...138

NOTES...164

INTRODUCTION

Welcome to the ultimate FC Barcelona quiz experience! This book is a celebration of the legendary football club, testing your knowledge on its rich history, iconic players, and unforgettable moments.

Whether you're a die-hard Barça fan or a casual observer of the beautiful game, prepare to be challenged and entertained as you delve into the fascinating world of FC Barcelona. From historic triumphs on the grand stage to the intricate details of the club's illustrious past, this book is designed to test your knowledge and celebrate the passion that makes Barcelona more than just a football team.

GENERAL QUIZ

How many times has FC Barcelona won the UEFA Champions League?
a) 4 times
b) 6 times
c) 5 times

Correct Answer: c)

Who is the all-time leading goal scorer for FC Barcelona?
a) Andrés Iniesta
b) Lionel Messi
c) Xavi Hernandez

Correct Answer: b)

In what year was FC Barcelona founded?

a) 1895

b) 1902

c) 1899

Correct Answer: c)

Which stadium is the home ground of FC Barcelona?

a) Anfield

b) Santiago Bernabéu

c) Camp Nou

Correct Answer: c)

Who is the current captain of FC Barcelona?

a) Gerard Piqué

b) Sergio Busquets

c) Lionel Messi

Correct Answer: c)

What does "Barça" mean, the popular nickname for FC Barcelona?

a) Victory

b) Passion

c) Short for Barcelona in Catalan

Correct Answer: c)

Which coach is credited with introducing the tiki-taka style of play at FC Barcelona?

a) Johan Cruyff

b) Pep Guardiola

c) Luis Enrique

Correct Answer: b)

Who holds the record for the most

consecutive La Liga appearances for FC Barcelona?

a) Xavi Hernandez

b) Lionel Messi

c) Carles Puyol

Correct Answer: c)

What is the name of the youth academy at FC Barcelona?

a) La Liga Academy

b) La Masia

c) Barça Youth

Correct Answer: b)

Which former player and manager is known as "The Wise Man" and played a crucial role in establishing FC Barcelona's youth development system?

a) Johan Cruyff

b) Louis van Gaal

c) Pep Guardiola

Correct Answer: a)

Which player famously wore the number 10 jersey for FC Barcelona before Lionel Messi?

a) Ronaldinho

b) Xavi Hernandez

c) Andres Iniesta

Correct Answer: a)

What is the capacity of Camp Nou, FC Barcelona's home stadium?

a) Approximately 85,000

b) Approximately 99,000

c) Approximately 110,000

Correct Answer: b)

Who is the top scorer in El Clásico matches in FC Barcelona's history?
a) Lionel Messi
b) Cristiano Ronaldo
c) Alfredo Di Stéfano

Correct Answer: a)

In which year did FC Barcelona sign the Brazilian forward Ronaldinho?
a) 2001
b) 2003
c) 2005

Correct Answer: b)

What is the name of the supporters' group known for their passionate support of FC Barcelona?

a) Boixos Nois

b) Barça Ultras

c) Culés Fanatics

Correct Answer: a)

Who is the oldest player to have played for FC Barcelona?

a) Luis Suárez

b) Henrik Larsson

c) Andoni Zubizarreta

Correct Answer: b)

How many times has FC Barcelona won the FIFA Club World Cup?

a) 2 times

b) 4 times

c) 3 times

Correct Answer: c)

In the summer of 2018, FC Barcelona signed Arturo Vidal from which Bundesliga club?

a) Bayern Munich

b) Borussia Dortmund

c) RB Leipzig

Correct Answer: a)

What is the name of the documentary series produced by Barça Studios that provides behind-the-scenes access to FC Barcelona?

a) Inside the Blaugrana

b) Barça Diaries

c) Matchday

Correct Answer: c)

Who is the first player to win six Ballon d'Or awards while playing for FC Barcelona?
a) Lionel Messi
b) Xavi Hernandez
c) Andrés Iniesta

Correct Answer: a)

Which former player is known for his iconic celebration, pointing to the sky, after scoring goals for FC Barcelona?
a) Samuel Eto'o
b) Luis Suárez
c) Thierry Henry

Correct Answer: a)

What is the official motto of FC Barcelona?

a) "More than a Club"

b) "Victory is Ours"

c) "Barça Forever"

Correct Answer: a)

FC Barcelona signed Ousmane Dembélé from which Bundesliga club in the summer of 2017?

a) Borussia Dortmund

b) Bayer Leverkusen

c) RB Leipzig

Correct Answer: a)

Which player won the Ballon d'Or while playing for FC Barcelona in 1994?

a) Romário

b) Ronaldo Nazário

c) Hristo Stoichkov

Correct Answer: c)

What is the name of the foundation established by FC Barcelona for social and humanitarian causes?

a) Barça Cares

b) Barça Foundation

c) Barça Aid

Correct Answer: b)

In which year did FC Barcelona first introduce a shirt sponsor?

a) 1984

b) 2006

c) 1992

Correct Answer: c)

Which player is known for his famous

"Hand of God" goal against England in the 1986 FIFA World Cup and also played for FC Barcelona?

a) Diego Maradona

b) Rivaldo

c) Ronaldinho

Correct Answer: a)

In the summer transfer window of 2020, FC Barcelona signed Miralem Pjanic from which Serie A club as part of a swap deal with Arthur Melo?

a) Juventus

b) Inter Milan

c) AC Milan

Correct Answer: a)

What is the capacity of the Mini Estadi,

the former home stadium of FC Barcelona B?

a) Approximately 8,000

b) Approximately 15,000

c) Approximately 20,000

Correct Answer: a)

Who is the record transfer signing for FC Barcelona as of the latest available information?

a) Ousmane Dembélé

b) Antoine Griezmann

c) Philippe Coutinho

Correct Answer: a)

What is the name of the club's mascot?

a) Barçito

b) Biruleta

c) Blau

Correct Answer: b)

In what year did FC Barcelona inaugurate Camp Nou?

a) 1957

b) 1965

c) 1974

Correct Answer: b)

In the summer of 2015, FC Barcelona signed Aleix Vidal from which La Liga club?

a) Sevilla

b) Valencia

c) Villarreal

Correct Answer: a)

Who is the top scorer in the history of El Clásico matches between FC Barcelona and Real Madrid?

a) Lionel Messi

b) Cristiano Ronaldo

c) Alfredo Di Stéfano

Correct Answer: a)

What is the name of the club's official fan magazine?

a) Blaugrana Magazine

b) Barça Forever

c) Barça Magazine

Correct Answer: c)

Which former player and manager is often referred to as the "Architect" of FC Barcelona's success in the 1990s?

a) Johan Cruyff

b) Louis van Gaal

c) Frank Rijkaard

Correct Answer: a)

How many times has FC Barcelona won the Copa del Rey?

a) 25 times

b) 31 times

c) 23 times

Correct Answer: b)

Jean-Clair Todibo, a young French defender, was signed by FC Barcelona in the winter transfer window of 2019 from which Ligue 1 club?

a) Lille

b) Toulouse

c) Lyon

Correct Answer: b)

Who is the president of FC Barcelona as of the latest information?

a) Joan Laporta

b) Josep Maria Bartomeu

c) Sandro Rosell

Correct Answer: a)

Which former player and coach is known for his "Total Football" philosophy and managed FC Barcelona in the late 1970s?

a) Johan Cruyff

b) Rinus Michels

c) Luis Suárez Miramontes

Correct Answer: b)

What is the name of the sports city where FC Barcelona's training facilities are located?

a) Ciutat Esportiva de Joan Gamper

b) Barça Training Grounds

c) Camp Nou Training Center

Correct Answer: a)

Who scored the winning goal for FC Barcelona in the 2006 UEFA Champions League final?

a) Samuel Eto'o

b) Ludovic Giuly

c) Juliano Belletti

Correct Answer: c)

How many times has FC Barcelona won the UEFA Super Cup?

a) 3 times

b) 5 times

c) 4 times

Correct Answer: c)

Which player has won the most Ballon d'Or awards while playing for FC Barcelona?

a) Xavi Hernandez

b) Andrés Iniesta

c) Lionel Messi

Correct Answer: c)

Who is the club's all-time assist leader?

a) Andrés Iniesta

b) Xavi Hernandez

c) Lionel Messi

Correct Answer: b)

Which midfielder is known for his iconic celebration, kissing his wedding ring, after scoring goals for FC Barcelona?

a) Andrés Iniesta

b) Sergio Busquets

c) Ivan Rakitić

Correct Answer: c)

What is the club's longest unbeaten streak in La Liga?

a) 31 matches

b) 39 matches

c) 44 matches

Correct Answer: c)

Who is the first player to score 500 goals for FC Barcelona?

a) Lionel Messi

b) Luis Suárez

c) Neymar

Correct Answer: a)

Which player holds the record for the most clean sheets for FC Barcelona?

a) Victor Valdés

b) Claudio Bravo

c) Marc-André ter Stegen

Correct Answer: a)

What is the total number of official competitions recognized by FC Barcelona?

a) 10

b) 15

c) 20

Correct Answer: b)

Which English club did FC Barcelona defeat in the 1992 European Cup final to claim their first Champions League title?

a) Manchester United

b) Liverpool

c) Arsenal

Correct Answer: c)

Who scored the first goal in the history of Camp Nou?

a) Luis Suárez Miramontes

b) László Kubala

c) Zoltán Czibor

Correct Answer: c)

Which player won the Ballon d'Or while playing for FC Barcelona in 1973?

a) Johan Cruyff

b) Luis Suárez Miramontes

c) Hristo Stoichkov

Correct Answer: b)

Who is the youngest player to have made a first-team appearance for FC Barcelona?

a) Bojan Krkić

b) Ansu Fati

c) Lionel Messi

Correct Answer: b)

In what year did FC Barcelona sign Johan Cruyff as a player?

a) 1973

b) 1976

c) 1970

Correct Answer: c)

What is the name of the youth tournament organized by FC Barcelona for under-12 teams from around the world?

a) Barça Cup

b) La Masia Trophy

c) Mediterranean International Cup

Correct Answer: c)

Who is the only player to have won the FIFA Club World Cup Golden Ball while representing FC Barcelona?

a) Lionel Messi

b) Xavi Hernandez

c) Luis Suárez

Correct Answer: b)

In what year did FC Barcelona establish the Barça Foundation?

a) 2005

b) 2010

c) 2008

Correct Answer: c)

Which former player is known as "The King of the Dribble" and played for FC Barcelona in the 1960s?

a) Ladislao Kubala

b) Luis Suárez Miramontes

c) Luis Suárez (Barcelona's 2020s player)

Correct Answer: a)

Who is the youngest goal scorer in the history of FC Barcelona?

a) Ansu Fati

b) Bojan Krkić

c) Lionel Messi

Correct Answer: b)

In which year did FC Barcelona establish the Barça B basketball team?

a) 1926

b) 1940

c) 1955

Correct Answer: c)

Which player scored the fastest goal in the history of FC Barcelona?

a) Thierry Henry

b) Hristo Stoichkov

c) Ludovic Giuly

Correct Answer: c)

Who is the current head coach of FC Barcelona?

a) Ronald Koeman

b) Xavi Hernandez

c) Pep Guardiola

Correct Answer: a)

What is the name of the club's anthem called?

a) Barça Hymn

b) Cant del Barça

c) Anthem of Blaugrana

Correct Answer: b)

Which player is known for his incredible goal-scoring record as a defender for FC Barcelona?

a) Dani Alves

b) Carles Puyol

c) Gerard Piqué

Correct Answer: a)

Who is the top scorer in El Clásico matches for FC Barcelona?

a) Lionel Messi

b) Luis Suárez

c) Neymar

Correct Answer: a)

In what year did FC Barcelona win their first European Cup Winners' Cup?

a) 1979

b) 1983

c) 1971

Correct Answer: c)

Which player is known for his incredible goal-scoring record as a defender for FC Barcelona?

a) Dani Alves

b) Carles Puyol

c) Gerard Piqué

Correct Answer: a)

What is the name of the organization founded by FC Barcelona to promote the club's values globally?

a) Barça Global

b) Barça Innovate

c) Barça Innovation Hub

Correct Answer: c)

Who is the all-time leading scorer in El Clásico matches for FC Barcelona?

a) Lionel Messi

b) Luis Suárez

c) Neymar

Correct Answer: a)

In what year did FC Barcelona establish the Barça Foundation?

a) 2005

b) 2010

c) 2008

Correct Answer: c)

Which former player and manager is known as "The Wise Man" and played a crucial role in establishing FC Barcelona's youth development system?

a) Johan Cruyff

b) Luis Enrique

c) Pep Guardiola

Correct Answer: a)

What is the total number of official competitions recognized by FC Barcelona?

a) 10

b) 15

c) 20

Correct Answer: b)

Which player has won the most Ballon d'Or awards while playing for FC Barcelona?

a) Xavi Hernandez

b) Andrés Iniesta

c) Lionel Messi

Correct Answer: c)

What is the name of the club's all-time assist leader?

a) Andrés Iniesta

b) Xavi Hernandez

c) Lionel Messi

Correct Answer: b)

Who is the first player to win six Ballon d'Or awards while playing for FC Barcelona?

a) Lionel Messi

b) Xavi Hernandez

c) Andrés Iniesta

Correct Answer: a)

What is the capacity of the Mini Estadi, the former home stadium of FC Barcelona B?

a) Approximately 8,000

b) Approximately 15,000

c) Approximately 20,000

Correct Answer: a)

Which Spanish king granted the "Royal" title to FC Barcelona in 1920?

a) King Alfonso XIII

b) King Juan Carlos I

c) King Felipe VI

Correct Answer: a)

Who was the coach of FC Barcelona when they won their first European Cup in 1992?

a) Johan Cruyff

b) Louis van Gaal

c) Pep Guardiola

Correct Answer: a)

Which former player is known as "The Wizard" and is considered one of the greatest midfielders in FC Barcelona's history?

a) Xavi Hernandez

b) Andrés Iniesta

c) Johan Cruyff

Correct Answer: b)

What is the name of the youth tournament organized by FC Barcelona for under-12 teams from around the world?

a) Barça Cup

b) La Masia Trophy

c) Mediterranean International Cup

Correct Answer: c)

Who scored the first goal in the history of Camp Nou?

a) Luis Suárez Miramontes

b) László Kubala

c) Zoltán Czibor

Correct Answer: c)

Which former player is known for his iconic celebration, kissing his wedding ring, after scoring goals for FC Barcelona?

a) Samuel Eto'o

b) Luis Suárez

c) Thierry Henry

Correct Answer: a)

Which goalkeeper has the most appearances for FC Barcelona?
a) Victor Valdés
b) Claudio Bravo
c) Marc-André ter Stegen

Correct Answer: a)

What is the name of the organization founded by FC Barcelona to promote the club's values globally?
a) Barça Global
b) Barça Innovate
c) Barça Innovation Hub

Correct Answer: c)

In which year did FC Barcelona win their first La Liga title?
a) 1925

b) 1935

c) 1945

Correct Answer: a)

Which Brazilian player is known for his spectacular goals and assists during his time at FC Barcelona?

a) Neymar

b) Ronaldinho

c) Rivaldo

Correct Answer: b)

What is the nickname of the supporters' group known for their passionate support of FC Barcelona?

a) Culés Ultras

b) Boixos Nois

c) Blaugrana Force

Correct Answer: b)

Who is the club's all-time leading scorer in domestic competitions?

a) Lionel Messi

b) César Rodríguez

c) Luis Suárez

Correct Answer: b)

What is the name of FC Barcelona's youth academy?

a) La Liga Academy

b) Barça B School

c) La Masia

Correct Answer: c)

Who is the only player to have won the FIFA Club World Cup Golden Ball while representing FC Barcelona?

a) Lionel Messi

b) Xavi Hernandez

c) Luis Suárez

Correct Answer: b)

In what year did FC Barcelona win their first FIFA Club World Cup?

a) 2007

b) 2009

c) 2011

Correct Answer: b)

What is the name of the sports city's stadium where FC Barcelona's youth teams play their matches?

a) Camp Nou

b) Mini Estadi

c) Estadi Johan Cruyff

Correct Answer: c)

Who is the only player to have won the Ballon d'Or while playing for FC Barcelona in 1994?

a) Romário

b) Ronaldo Nazário

c) Hristo Stoichkov

Correct Answer: c)

Which French defender formed a formidable partnership with Carles Puyol in FC Barcelona's defense in the 2000s?

a) Éric Abidal

b) Lilian Thuram

c) Samuel Umtiti

Correct Answer: a)

Who is the club's all-time leading scorer in domestic competitions?
a) Lionel Messi
b) Luis Suárez
c) César Rodríguez

Correct Answer: c)

What is the nickname of the supporters' group known for their passionate support of FC Barcelona?
a) Culés Ultras
b) Boixos Nois
c) Blaugrana Force

Correct Answer: b)

Which player holds the record for the

most assists in a single La Liga season for FC Barcelona?

a) Xavi Hernandez

b) Andrés Iniesta

c) Lionel Messi

Correct Answer: a)

In what year did FC Barcelona win their first FIFA Club World Cup?

a) 2007

b) 2009

c) 2011

Correct Answer: b)

Who is the top scorer in the history of El Clásico matches between FC Barcelona and Real Madrid?

a) Lionel Messi

b) Cristiano Ronaldo

c) Alfredo Di Stéfano

Correct Answer: a)

What is the name of the sports city's stadium where FC Barcelona's youth teams play their matches?

a) Camp Nou

b) Mini Estadi

c) Estadi Johan Cruyff

Correct Answer: c)

Which player won the Ballon d'Or while playing for FC Barcelona in 1994?

a) Romário

b) Ronaldo Nazário

c) Hristo Stoichkov

Correct Answer: c)

Who is the only player to have won the FIFA Club World Cup Golden Ball while representing FC Barcelona?

a) Lionel Messi

b) Xavi Hernandez

c) Luis Suárez

Correct Answer: b)

In what year did FC Barcelona establish the Barça Foundation?

a) 2005

b) 2010

c) 2008

Correct Answer: c)

Which former player and manager is known as "The Wise Man" and played a crucial role in establishing FC

Barcelona's youth development system?

a) Johan Cruyff

b) Luis Enrique

c) Pep Guardiola

Correct Answer: a)

Who is the only goalkeeper to have won the Ballon d'Or while playing for FC Barcelona?

a) Victor Valdés

b) Andoni Zubizarreta

c) Marc-André ter Stegen

Correct Answer: b)

Which Brazilian striker played a crucial role in FC Barcelona's treble-winning season in 2014-2015?

a) Ronaldo Nazário

b) Romário

c) Neymar

Correct Answer: c)

In what year did FC Barcelona sign Luis Suárez from Liverpool?

a) 2013

b) 2014

c) 2015

Correct Answer: b)

What is the name of the official mascot of FC Barcelona?

a) Biruleta

b) Boixos

c) Barçito

Correct Answer: a)

Which legendary Dutch midfielder played for FC Barcelona and was part of the "Dream Team" under Johan Cruyff?

a) Frank Rijkaard

b) Ronald Koeman

c) Marco van Basten

Correct Answer: b)

Who scored the decisive goal in FC Barcelona's 1-0 win over Manchester United in the 2009 UEFA Champions League final?

a) Andrés Iniesta

b) Lionel Messi

c) Xavi Hernandez

Correct Answer: a)

What is the nickname of FC Barcelona's women's football team?

a) Barça Ladies

b) Blaugrana Women

c) Barça Femení

Correct Answer: c)

Which former Dutch international played as a goalkeeper for FC Barcelona and is known for his penalty-saving prowess?

a) Edwin van der Sar

b) Jasper Cillessen

c) Victor Valdés

Correct Answer: c)

Who is the all-time leading scorer for FC Barcelona in UEFA Champions

League/European Cup competitions?

a) Lionel Messi

b) Xavi Hernandez

c) Luis Suárez

Correct Answer: a)

What is the name of FC Barcelona's training ground?

a) Camp Nou Training Center

b) La Masia

c) Ciutat Esportiva Joan Gamper

Correct Answer: c)

Which Portuguese midfielder, often referred to as "The Maestro," played for FC Barcelona in the late 1990s and early 2000s?

a) Deco

b) Luís Figo

c) Rui Costa

Correct Answer: a)

In what year did FC Barcelona sign the Argentine forward Javier Saviola?

a) 2001

b) 2003

c) 2005

Correct Answer: a)

Which former FC Barcelona player and manager is nicknamed "Tata"?

a) Tito Vilanova

b) Luis Enrique

c) Gerardo Martino

Correct Answer: c)

What is the name of the trophy awarded to the winner of the friendly match between FC Barcelona and Espanyol known as the "Derbi Barceloní"?

a) Trofeu Joan Gamper

b) Trofeu Ciutat de Barcelona

c) Trofeu Pichichi

Correct Answer: b)

Which player scored the winning goal for FC Barcelona in the 2006 UEFA Champions League final?

a) Samuel Eto'o

b) Ludovic Giuly

c) Juliano Belletti

Correct Answer: c)

Who is the current president of FC Barcelona as of the latest available information?

a) Joan Laporta

b) Josep Maria Bartomeu

c) Sandro Rosell

Correct Answer: a)

Which player, known for his powerful left foot, scored a stunning free-kick goal for FC Barcelona in the 2006 UEFA Champions League final?

a) Ronaldinho

b) Deco

c) Ronaldinho

Correct Answer: b)

In what year did FC Barcelona win

their first La Liga title after the Spanish Civil War?

a) 1947

b) 1950

c) 1952

Correct Answer: a)

Which Uruguayan forward formed a lethal attacking trio with Lionel Messi and Neymar at FC Barcelona?

a) Luis Suárez

b) Diego Forlán

c) Edinson Cavani

Correct Answer: a)

What is the nickname of FC Barcelona's veteran midfielder who is known for his passing ability and vision?

a) Sergio Busquets

b) Ivan Rakitić

c) Xavi Hernandez

Correct Answer: a)

Which Dutch midfielder, also known as the "Flying Dutchman," played for FC Barcelona and was a key figure in Johan Cruyff's Dream Team?

a) Edgar Davids

b) Marc Overmars

c) Ronald de Boer

Correct Answer: b)

In what year did FC Barcelona sign the Spanish midfielder Thiago Alcântara, who later became a key player for the club?

a) 2008

b) 2009

c) 2010

Correct Answer: b)

Who is the all-time leading scorer for FC Barcelona in the UEFA Champions League?

a) Lionel Messi

b) Samuel Eto'o

c) Rivaldo

Correct Answer: a)

What is the name of the annual award presented by FC Barcelona to the best player in the first team, as voted on by the fans?

a) Player of the Season

b) Golden Boot

c) Barça Fans' Award

Correct Answer: c)

Which former FC Barcelona player and manager is often referred to as "Tito"?

a) Tito Vilanova

b) Luis Enrique

c) Gerardo Martino

Correct Answer: a)

What is the name of the foundation established by FC Barcelona for social and humanitarian causes?

a) Barça Cares

b) Barça Foundation

c) Barça Aid

Correct Answer: b)

Which Brazilian forward, known for his flair and creativity, played for FC Barcelona in the early 2000s?

a) Rivaldo

b) Ronaldo Nazário

c) Ronaldinho

Correct Answer: a)

In what year did FC Barcelona sign the Argentine goalkeeper Juan Román Riquelme?

a) 1997

b) 1999

c) 2001

Correct Answer: a)

Who is the current captain of FC Barcelona Women's team?

a) Alexia Putella

b) Vicky Losada

c) Marta Torrejón

Correct Answer: a)

Which former Dutch international and Barcelona player is nicknamed "The Hunter" and is known for his goal-scoring prowess?

a) Patrick Kluivert

b) Ruud Gullit

c) Marco van Basten

Correct Answer: a)

In what year did FC Barcelona sign the Croatian midfielder Ivan Rakitić?

a) 2012

b) 2014

c) 2016

Correct Answer: b)

Who is the only player to have won the Golden Foot award while representing FC Barcelona?

a) Lionel Messi

b) Xavi Hernandez

c) Andrés Iniesta

Correct Answer: a)

What is the name of the stadium that served as FC Barcelona's home before the construction of Camp Nou?

a) Camp de Les Corts

b) Camp de la Indústria

c) Camp de la Maternitat

Correct Answer: a)

Which former FC Barcelona player is known for his role as the club's sporting director and later as the president of La Liga?

a) Joan Laporta

b) Sandro Rosell

c) Javier Tebas

Correct Answer: c)

In what year did FC Barcelona sign the French winger Ousmane Dembélé?

a) 2016

b) 2017

c) 2018

Correct Answer: b)

What is the name of the award presented to the top scorer of La Liga each season?

a) Pichichi Trophy

b) Golden Boot

c) La Liga Top Scorer Award

Correct Answer: a)

Who is the all-time leading scorer in official competitions for FC Barcelona Women's team?

a) Alexia Putella

b) Marta Torrejón

c) Jenni Hermoso

Correct Answer: c)

Which former FC Barcelona player and manager is nicknamed "Lucho"?

a) Luis Enrique

b) Pep Guardiola

c) Frank Rijkaard

Correct Answer: a)

In what year did FC Barcelona win their first UEFA Cup Winners' Cup?

a) 1979

b) 1983

c) 1971

Correct Answer: c)

What is the name of the player development program established by FC Barcelona to scout and nurture young talents?

a) Barça Academy

b) La Masia

c) Barça Youth Project

Correct Answer: b)

Which Dutch midfielder, known for his versatility and passing ability, played for FC Barcelona in the 2000s?

a) Mark van Bommel

b) Edgar Davids

c) Phillip Cocu

Correct Answer: c)

In what year did FC Barcelona sign the Spanish midfielder Sergio Busquets?

a) 2007

b) 2008

c) 2009

Correct Answer: b)

Who is the only player to have scored a hat-trick in an El Clásico match in the 21st century for FC Barcelona?

a) Lionel Messi

b) Luis Suárez

c) Neymar

Correct Answer: a)

What is the name of the club's official anthem, often played before home matches at Camp Nou?

a) Barça Hymn

b) Cant del Barça

c) Barça Anthem

Correct Answer: b)

Which former FC Barcelona player and manager is known for his role in the "Wembley Goal" during the 1992 UEFA Champions League final?

a) Johan Cruyff

b) Ronald Koeman

c) Hristo Stoichkov

Correct Answer: b)

In what year did FC Barcelona sign the Brazilian full-back Dani Alves?

a) 2006

b) 2008

c) 2009

Correct Answer: b)

FC Barcelona signed Martin Braithwaite in the winter transfer window of 2020 from which La Liga club as an emergency signing?

a) Leganés

b) Espanyol

c) Getafe

Correct Answer: a)

Who is the current captain of FC Barcelona Men's team?
a) Lionel Messi
b) Gerard Piqué
c) Sergio Busquets

Correct Answer: b)

What is the name of the competition that features FC Barcelona's youth teams and other European youth academies?
a) UEFA Youth League
b) NextGen Series
c) La Liga Juvenil

Correct Answer: a)

Which English club did FC Barcelona defeat in the 2015 UEFA Champions League final to secure their fifth European Cup title?

a) Manchester United

b) Chelsea

c) Arsenal

Correct Answer: b)

What is the nickname of the supporters' group known for their passionate support of FC Barcelona Women's team?

a) Barça Ladies Ultras

b) Boixos Nois Femení

c) Curva Femenina

Correct Answer: b)

Who is the current all-time leading scorer for FC Barcelona in the UEFA Champions League?
a) Lionel Messi
b) Samuel Eto'o
c) Neymar

Correct Answer: a)

In what year did FC Barcelona win their first treble, securing the La Liga, Copa del Rey, and UEFA Champions League titles in a single season?
a) 2007-2008
b) 2008-2009
c) 2009-2010

Correct Answer: b)

Which Brazilian defender, known for his

solid defensive skills, played for FC Barcelona in the 2000s?

a) Maxwell

b) Lucio

c) Edmilson

Correct Answer: a)

What is the name of the former FC Barcelona player who serves as the club's ambassador and is considered one of the greatest midfielders in football history?

a) Johan Cruyff

b) Xavi Hernandez

c) Andrés Iniesta

Correct Answer: c)

In what year did FC Barcelona sign the

Uruguayan striker Luis Suárez?

a) 2012

b) 2013

c) 2014

Correct Answer: c)

Who is the current coach of FC Barcelona Women's team?

a) Lluís Cortés

b) Xavi Hernandez

c) Ronald Koeman

Correct Answer: a)

What is the name of the friendly competition between FC Barcelona and Bayern Munich known as the "Joan Gamper Trophy"?

a) Barça-Bayern Classic

b) Gamper Cup

c) Friendship Cup

Correct Answer: b)

Which former player is known for his iconic celebration, pointing to the sky, after scoring goals for FC Barcelona?

a) Pedro Rodríguez

b) David Villa

c) Alexis Sánchez

Correct Answer: a)

What is the name of FC Barcelona's official mascot?

a) Biruleta

b) Barçito

c) Blaugrana Bear

Correct Answer: a)

Who is the only player to have won the Golden Foot award while representing FC Barcelona?

a) Lionel Messi

b) Xavi Hernandez

c) Andrés Iniesta

Correct Answer: a)

Which former FC Barcelona player is often referred to as "The Beast" and was known for his physical style of play as a midfielder?

a) Seydou Keita

b) Yaya Touré

c) Javier Mascherano

Correct Answer: b)

In what year did FC Barcelona sign the

Chilean goalkeeper Claudio Bravo?

a) 2013

b) 2014

c) 2015

Correct Answer: c)

Who holds the record for the most appearances in official competitions for FC Barcelona?

a) Lionel Messi

b) Xavi Hernandez

c) Andrés Iniesta

Correct Answer: a)

What is the name of FC Barcelona's official magazine, providing news and insights about the club?

a) Barça Insider

b) Blaugrana Digest

c) Barça Magazine

Correct Answer: c)

Which Brazilian midfielder, known for his flair and skill, played for FC Barcelona in the early 2000s?

a) Ronaldinho

b) Rivaldo

c) Kaká

Correct Answer: b)

In what year did FC Barcelona sign the French defender Samuel Umtiti?

a) 2015

b) 2016

c) 2017

Correct Answer: b)

Who is the current captain of FC Barcelona Women's team?

a) Alexia Putella

b) Vicky Losada

c) Marta Torrejón

Correct Answer: a)

What is the nickname of the supporters' group known for their passionate support of FC Barcelona Men's team?

a) Culés Ultras

b) Boixos Nois

c) Blaugrana Force

Correct Answer: b)

In what year did FC Barcelona sign the Dutch midfielder Frenkie de Jong?

a) 2017

b) 2018

c) 2019

Correct Answer: c)

Which former FC Barcelona player is known as "The Flash" due to his incredible speed on the pitch?

a) Thierry Henry

b) Samuel Eto'o

c) Ludovic Giuly

Correct Answer: c)

Who is the all-time leading scorer for FC Barcelona in the Copa del Rey?

a) Lionel Messi

b) César Rodríguez

c) Luis Suárez

Correct Answer: a)

In what year did FC Barcelona sign the Spanish forward David Villa?

a) 2009

b) 2010

c) 2011

Correct Answer: a)

Which former FC Barcelona player and coach is nicknamed "The Professor" for his tactical acumen and coaching philosophy?

a) Pep Guardiola

b) Luis Enrique

c) Tito Vilanova

Correct Answer: a)

What is the name of FC Barcelona's official online store where fans can purchase club merchandise?

a) Barça Shop

b) Blaugrana Store

c) FC Barcelona Megastore

Correct Answer: c)

Which Brazilian midfielder played alongside Ronaldinho and Deco in FC Barcelona's midfield during the mid-2000s?

a) Anderson

b) Edmilson

c) Belletti

Correct Answer: b)

In what year did FC Barcelona win their first European Cup?

a) 1958

b) 1961

c) 1965

Correct Answer: b)

Who is the current president of FC Barcelona Women's team?

a) Joan Laporta

b) Carles Tusquets

c) Maria Teixidor

Correct Answer: c)

What is the name of the former FC Barcelona player who serves as the club's director of football and is responsible for managing player transfers?

a) Andoni Zubizarreta

b) Eric Abidal

c) Guillermo Amor

Correct Answer: b)

In what year did FC Barcelona win their first Copa del Rey title?
a) 1910
b) 1912
c) 1914

Correct Answer: b)

Which former FC Barcelona player and manager is known for introducing the revolutionary "tiki-taka" style of play?
a) Johan Cruyff
b) Pep Guardiola
c) Louis van Gaal

Correct Answer: b)

What is the name of the stadium where FC Barcelona's youth teams play their matches?

a) Mini Estadi

b) Ciutat Esportiva Joan Gamper

c) Camp Nou B

Correct Answer: b)

In what year did FC Barcelona sign the Dutch goalkeeper Jasper Cillessen?

a) 2015

b) 2016

c) 2017

Correct Answer: b)

Who is the only player to have won the FIFA World Player of the Year award while representing FC Barcelona?

a) Ronaldinho

b) Lionel Messi

c) Xavi Hernandez

Correct Answer: b)

What is the name of the official FC Barcelona podcast that provides fans with interviews, analysis, and behind-the-scenes content?

a) Barça Talks

b) Blaugrana Banter

c) The Barça Podcast

Correct Answer: c)

Which former FC Barcelona player is known for his role as a television pundit and commentator, providing insights on football matches?

a) Carles Puyol

b) Xavi Hernandez

c) Hristo Stoichkov

Correct Answer: a)

In what year did FC Barcelona win their first FIFA Club World Cup?

a) 2007

b) 2009

c) 2011

Correct Answer: b)

Who is the current captain of FC Barcelona Men's team?

a) Lionel Messi

b) Gerard Piqué

c) Sergio Busquets

Correct Answer: b)

What is the name of the former FC Barcelona player who served as the club's sporting director and later as the president of the European Club Association (ECA)?

a) Joan Laporta

b) Sandro Rosell

c) Josep Maria Bartomeu

Correct Answer: b)

In what year did FC Barcelona sign the French defender Clément Lenglet?

a) 2017

b) 2018

c) 2019

Correct Answer: b)

Which former Dutch international

played as a midfielder for FC Barcelona and was part of the Dream Team under Johan Cruyff?

a) Ronald Koeman

b) Frank Rijkaard

c) Edgar Davids

Correct Answer: a)

What is the name of the prestigious friendly tournament organized by FC Barcelona every summer, featuring top international clubs?

a) Barcelona Trophy

b) Joan Gamper Trophy

c) Camp Nou Cup

Correct Answer: b)

In what year did FC Barcelona win

their first Supercopa de España title?

a) 1983

b) 1985

c) 1991

Correct Answer: a)

Which former FC Barcelona player and manager is nicknamed "The Boss" and played a crucial role in establishing the modern success of the club?

a) Johan Cruyff

b) Pep Guardiola

c) Luis Enrique

Correct Answer: b)

What is the name of the award presented to the best goalkeeper in La Liga each season?

a) Zamora Trophy

b) Golden Glove Award

c) Pichichi Trophy

Correct Answer: a)

Which Dutch forward, known for his goal-scoring ability, played for FC Barcelona in the late 1990s and early 2000s?

a) Patrick Kluivert

b) Dennis Bergkamp

c) Ruud van Nistelrooy

Correct Answer: a)

In what year did FC Barcelona win their first UEFA Super Cup?

a) 1992

b) 1997

c) 2000

Correct Answer: b)

Who is the current head coach of FC Barcelona Men's team?

a) Ronald Koeman

b) Xavi Hernandez

c) Luis Enrique

Correct Answer: a)

What is the name of the official FC Barcelona TV channel that provides exclusive content, interviews, and match highlights?

a) Barça TV

b) Blaugrana Channel

c) Camp Nou Network

Correct Answer: a)

In what year did FC Barcelona sign the Croatian midfielder Ivan Perišić?

a) 2018

b) 2019

c) 2020

Correct Answer: c)

Which former FC Barcelona player is known for his nickname "The Flea" and is considered one of the greatest footballers of all time?

a) Diego Maradona

b) Lionel Messi

c) Johan Cruyff

Correct Answer: b)

In what year did FC Barcelona establish their official supporters' club, known as

"Penya Blaugrana"?

a) 1915

b) 1920

c) 1930

Correct Answer: a)

Which Uruguayan forward, known for his goal-scoring prowess, played for FC Barcelona in the late 1960s and early 1970s?

a) Enrique Castro "Quini"

b) Ladislao Kubala

c) Luis Suárez Miramontes

Correct Answer: c)

What is the name of the competition where FC Barcelona's youth teams compete against other Spanish clubs' youth academies?

a) La Liga Juvenil

b) Copa del Rey Juvenil

c) Segunda División B Juvenil

Correct Answer: a)

In what year did FC Barcelona sign the Brazilian defender Dani Alves?

a) 2006

b) 2007

c) 2008

Correct Answer: c)

Who is the only goalkeeper to have won the Ballon d'Or while playing for FC Barcelona?

a) Victor Valdés

b) Andoni Zubizarreta

c) Marc-André ter Stegen

Correct Answer: b)

What is the name of FC Barcelona's youth academy, renowned for developing talented players such as Lionel Messi and Xavi Hernandez?

a) Barça Academy

b) La Masia

c) Camp Nou Youth Center

Correct Answer: b)

In what year did FC Barcelona win their first-ever European Cup Winners' Cup?

a) 1979

b) 1982

c) 1989

Correct Answer: c)

Which French center-back formed a formidable defensive partnership with Gerard Piqué during FC Barcelona's successful era under Pep Guardiola?

a) Éric Abidal

b) Samuel Umtiti

c) Lilian Thuram

Correct Answer: a)

What is the name of the annual award presented by FC Barcelona to the best player in the first team, as voted on by the players themselves?

a) Golden Boot

b) Pichichi Trophy

c) Barça Players' Award

Correct Answer: c)

Who is the current all-time leading scorer for FC Barcelona in La Liga?

a) Lionel Messi

b) César Rodríguez

c) Luis Suárez

Correct Answer: a)

In what year did FC Barcelona sign the Spanish forward Pedro Rodríguez?

a) 2007

b) 2008

c) 2009

Correct Answer: b)

In the summer of 2017, FC Barcelona signed Paulinho from which Chinese

Super League club, making a surprising move for the Brazilian midfielder?

a) Shanghai SIPG

b) Beijing Guoan

c) Guangzhou Evergrande

Correct Answer: c)

Which former FC Barcelona player and manager is known for his iconic role as a sweeper during his playing days and later as a coach who implemented the "Total Football" philosophy?

a) Johan Cruyff

b) Frank Rijkaard

c) Louis van Gaal

Correct Answer: a)

What is the name of the official FC

Barcelona anthem played before every home match at Camp Nou?

a) Barça Anthem

b) Camp Nou Hymn

c) Cant del Barça

Correct Answer: c)

In what year did FC Barcelona sign the French midfielder Ludovic Giuly?

a) 2004

b) 2005

c) 2006

Correct Answer: a)

Who holds the record for the most appearances as a captain for FC Barcelona Men's team?

a) Xavi Hernandez

b) Carles Puyol

c) Lionel Messi

Correct Answer: b)

Which Dutch midfielder, known for his passing accuracy and vision, played a key role in FC Barcelona's success under Pep Guardiola?

a) Mark van Bommel

b) Edgar Davids

c) Xavi Hernandez

Correct Answer: c)

In what year did FC Barcelona win their first FIFA World Club Cup title?

a) 2008

b) 2009

c) 2010

Correct Answer: b)

What is the name of the trophy awarded to the La Liga team that finishes the season with the best fair play record?

a) Fair Play Trophy

b) Fair Play Award

c) Zamora Trophy

Correct Answer: b)

Which former FC Barcelona player and manager is known for his role as a center-back and later as a coach who led the team to multiple domestic and international titles?

a) Luis Enrique

b) Frank Rijkaard

c) Pep Guardiola

Correct Answer: b)

Who is the current captain of FC Barcelona Men's team?

a) Lionel Messi

b) Gerard Piqué

c) Sergio Busquets

Correct Answer: b)

In what year did FC Barcelona sign the Spanish midfielder Thiago Alcântara, who later became a key player for the club?

a) 2008

b) 2009

c) 2010

Correct Answer: b)

Which former FC Barcelona player and manager is nicknamed "Tata"?

a) Tito Vilanova

b) Luis Enrique

c) Gerardo Martino

Correct Answer: c)

What is the name of the trophy awarded to the winner of the friendly match between FC Barcelona and Espanyol known as the "Derbi Barceloní"?

a) Trofeu Joan Gamper

b) Trofeu Ciutat de Barcelona

c) Trofeu Pichichi

Correct Answer: b)

Which player scored the winning goal

for FC Barcelona in the 2006 UEFA Champions League final?

a) Samuel Eto'o

b) Ludovic Giuly

c) Juliano Belletti

Correct Answer: c)

Who is the current president of FC Barcelona as of the latest available information (2024)?

a) Joan Laporta

b) Josep Maria Bartomeu

c) Sandro Rosell

Correct Answer: a)

Which player, known for his powerful left foot, scored a stunning free-kick goal for FC Barcelona in the 2006

UEFA Champions League final?

a) Ronaldinho

b) Deco

c) Ronaldinho

Correct Answer: b)

In what year did FC Barcelona win their first La Liga title after the Spanish Civil War?

a) 1947

b) 1950

c) 1952

Correct Answer: a)

Which Uruguayan forward formed a lethal attacking trio with Lionel Messi and Neymar at FC Barcelona?

a) Luis Suárez

b) Diego Forlán

c) Edinson Cavani

Correct Answer: a)

What is the nickname of FC Barcelona's veteran midfielder who is known for his passing ability and vision?

a) Sergio Busquets

b) Ivan Rakitić

c) Xavi Hernandez

Correct Answer: a)

Which Portuguese midfielder, often referred to as "The Maestro," played for FC Barcelona in the late 1990s and early 2000s?

a) Deco

b) Luís Figo

c) Rui Costa

Correct Answer: a)

In what year did FC Barcelona sign the Spanish midfielder Sergio Busquets?

a) 2006

b) 2008

c) 2009

Correct Answer: b)

Who is the current captain of FC Barcelona Women's team?

a) Alexia Putella

b) Vicky Losada

c) Marta Torrejón

Correct Answer: a)

What is the name of the foundation

established by FC Barcelona for social and humanitarian causes?

a) Barça Cares

b) Barça Foundation

c) Barça Aid

Correct Answer: b)

Which Brazilian forward, known for his flair and creativity, played for FC Barcelona in the early 2000s?

a) Rivaldo

b) Ronaldo Nazário

c) Ronaldinho

Correct Answer: a)

In what year did FC Barcelona sign the Argentine goalkeeper Juan Román Riquelme?

a) 1997

b) 1999

c) 2001

Correct Answer: a)

What is the name of the official magazine published by FC Barcelona, featuring news, interviews, and articles about the club?

a) Barça Mag

b) Blaugrana News

c) Barça Magazine

Correct Answer: c)

Who is the all-time leading scorer for FC Barcelona Women's team in official competitions?

a) Alexia Putella

b) Marta Torrejón

c) Jenni Hermoso

Correct Answer: c)

Which former FC Barcelona player and manager is often referred to as "Lucho"?

a) Luis Enrique

b) Pep Guardiola

c) Frank Rijkaard

Correct Answer: a)

What is the name of the annual award presented by FC Barcelona to the best player in the first team, as voted on by the fans?

a) Player of the Season

b) Golden Boot

c) Barça Fans' Award

Correct Answer: c)

Which Dutch midfielder, also known as the "Flying Dutchman," played for FC Barcelona and was a key figure in Johan Cruyff's Dream Team?
a) Edgar Davids
b) Marc Overmars
c) Ronald de Boer

Correct Answer: b)

In what year did FC Barcelona sign the Spanish midfielder Thiago Motta?
a) 1999
b) 2000
c) 2001

Correct Answer: b)

Who is the current head coach of FC Barcelona Women's team?

a) Lluís Cortés

b) Xavi Hernandez

c) Ronald Koeman

Correct Answer: a)

What is the name of the friendly competition between FC Barcelona and Juventus known as the "Joan Gamper Trophy"?

a) Barça-Juve Challenge

b) Gamper Cup

c) Trophy of Champions

Correct Answer: b)

Which former FC Barcelona player and coach is known for his role as a goalkeeper and later as the director of football at the club?

a) Andoni Zubizarreta

b) Victor Valdés

c) José Ramón Alexanko

Correct Answer: a)

In what year did FC Barcelona sign the Brazilian defender Maxwell?

a) 2008

b) 2009

c) 2010

Correct Answer: b)

What is the name of the competition that features FC Barcelona's youth teams competing against other international youth academies?

a) UEFA Youth Cup

b) NextGen Series

c) La Masia Cup

Correct Answer: b)

Who is the only player to have won the FIFA World Player of the Year award while representing FC Barcelona Women's team?

a) Lieke Martens

b) Alexia Putella

c) Marta Torrejón

Correct Answer: a)

Which Argentine forward, known for his goal-scoring prowess and partnership with Lionel Messi, played for FC Barcelona in the late 2000s?

a) Gonzalo Higuaín

b) Carlos Tevez

c) Ezequiel Lavezzi

Correct Answer: a)

What is the name of the former FC Barcelona player who is widely regarded as the club's greatest goalkeeper and is nicknamed "El Muro" (The Wall)?

a) Victor Valdés

b) Andoni Zubizarreta

c) Carles Puyol

Correct Answer: b)

In what year did FC Barcelona sign the Spanish defender Jordi Alba?

a) 2009

b) 2010

c) 2012

Correct Answer: c)

Which former FC Barcelona player and manager is known for his tenure during the "Dream Team" era and for introducing the concept of "Total Football" at the club?

a) Johan Cruyff

b) Pep Guardiola

c) Luis Enrique

Correct Answer: a)

In what year did FC Barcelona sign the French defender Éric Abidal?

a) 2007

b) 2008

c) 2009

Correct Answer: b)

Who is the all-time leading assist provider for FC Barcelona in La Liga?

a) Xavi Hernandez

b) Lionel Messi

c) Andrés Iniesta

Correct Answer: a)

What is the name of the former FC Barcelona player who is known for his remarkable ability to score goals from free-kicks and is often referred to as "The Beast"?

a) Lionel Messi

b) Luis Suárez

c) Ronaldinho

Correct Answer: c)

In what year did FC Barcelona win their first UEFA Cup Winners' Cup?

a) 1970

b) 1971

c) 1979

Correct Answer: a)

Which former FC Barcelona player is known for his role as a forward and his impressive goal-scoring record, earning him the nickname "The Condor"?

a) César Rodríguez

b) Kubala

c) László Kubala

Correct Answer: a)

What is the name of the trophy awarded to the top scorer of La Liga each season?
a) Pichichi Trophy
b) Golden Boot
c) Zamora Trophy

Correct Answer: a)

Which Dutch goalkeeper joined FC Barcelona in the summer of 2016 as a backup to Marc-André ter Stegen?
a) Jasper Cillessen
b) Maarten Stekelenburg
c) Tim Krul

Correct Answer: a)

In what year did FC Barcelona win their first Inter-Cities Fairs Cup, a precursor to the UEFA Cup and UEFA Europa League?

a) 1958

b) 1959

c) 1960

Correct Answer: b)

Which former FC Barcelona player and manager is known for his contributions to the club's youth development and coaching philosophy, emphasizing player education?

a) Xavi Hernandez

b) Andrés Iniesta

c) Pep Guardiola

Correct Answer: c)

Who is the only goalkeeper to have won

the UEFA Best Player in Europe Award while playing for FC Barcelona?

a) Victor Valdés

b) Marc-André ter Stegen

c) Claudio Bravo

Correct Answer: b)

In the summer of 2007, FC Barcelona signed Thierry Henry from which English Premier League club?

a) Arsenal

b) Manchester United

c) Chelsea

Correct Answer: a)

What is the name of the former FC Barcelona player and coach who is often regarded as one of the greatest

midfielders in football history and is known for his elegance on the ball?
a) Andrés Iniesta
b) Xavi Hernandez
c) Luis Suárez

Correct Answer: b)

In what year did FC Barcelona sign the Chilean goalkeeper Claudio Bravo?
a) 2013
b) 2014
c) 2015

Correct Answer: a)

Which Spanish midfielder joined FC Barcelona from Villarreal in the summer of 2002 and played a key role in the team's midfield for several years?

a) Marcos Senna

b) Juan Román Riquelme

c) Xavi Hernández

Correct Answer: c)

Who is the only player to have won the UEFA Best Player in Europe Award while representing FC Barcelona Women's team?

a) Lieke Martens

b) Alexia Putella

c) Jennifer Hermoso

Correct Answer: a)

What is the name of the former FC Barcelona player and manager who is often referred to as "The Dreamer" and played a crucial role in the club's success in the late 1980s and early 1990s?

a) Johan Cruyff

b) Luis Enrique

c) Johan Neeskens

Correct Answer: a)

In what year did FC Barcelona sign the Croatian midfielder Ivan Rakitić?

a) 2013

b) 2014

c) 2015

Correct Answer: b)

Which former FC Barcelona player is known for his nickname "The Flea" and is considered one of the greatest footballers of all time?

a) Diego Maradona

b) Lionel Messi

c) Johan Cruyff

Correct Answer: b)

Which Brazilian midfielder joined FC Barcelona in the summer of 1986 from Flamengo, becoming a creative force in the team's midfield?

a) Zico

b) Sócrates

c) Romário

Correct Answer: a)

What is the name of the competition where FC Barcelona's youth teams compete against other European youth academies?

a) UEFA Youth League

b) La Liga Juvenil

c) NextGen Series

Correct Answer: a)

Who is the current captain of FC Barcelona Men's team?

a) Lionel Messi

b) Gerard Piqué

c) Sergio Busquets

Correct Answer: b)

In what year did FC Barcelona sign the Brazilian forward Neymar?

a) 2012

b) 2013

c) 2014

Correct Answer: b)

Which former FC Barcelona player is known for his role as a versatile midfielder and his involvement in multiple successful eras at the club?
a) Andrés Iniesta
b) Luis Suárez
c) Seydou Keita

Correct Answer: c)

What is the name of the official FC Barcelona supporters' anthem, traditionally sung by the fans before and during matches?
a) Barça Anthem
b) Cant del Barça
c) Barça Hymn

Correct Answer: b)

In what year did FC Barcelona sign the Dutch goalkeeper Jasper Cillessen?

a) 2015

b) 2016

c) 2017

Correct Answer: a)

Who is the current president of FC Barcelona Women's team?

a) Joan Laporta

b) Carles Tusquets

c) Maria Teixidor

Correct Answer: c)

What is the name of the former FC Barcelona player who serves as the club's director of football and is responsible for managing player transfers?

a) Andoni Zubizarreta

b) Eric Abidal

c) Guillermo Amor

Correct Answer: b)

In what year did FC Barcelona sign the French defender Clément Lenglet?

a) 2017

b) 2018

c) 2019

Correct Answer: b)

Who is the all-time leading scorer for FC Barcelona in the Copa del Rey?

a) Lionel Messi

b) César Rodríguez

c) Luis Suárez

Correct Answer: a)

In what year did FC Barcelona sign the Spanish forward David Villa?
a) 2009
b) 2010
c) 2011

Correct Answer: a)

What is the name of the former FC Barcelona player and manager who is nicknamed "The Professor" for his tactical acumen and coaching philosophy?
a) Pep Guardiola
b) Luis Enrique
c) Tito Vilanova

Correct Answer: a)

Which Brazilian midfielder, known for his flair and skill, played for FC Barcelona in the early 2000s?

a) Ronaldinho

b) Rivaldo

c) Kaká

Correct Answer: b)

In what year did FC Barcelona sign the French defender Samuel Umtiti?

a) 2015

b) 2016

c) 2017

Correct Answer: b)

What is the name of the stadium where FC Barcelona's youth teams play their matches?

a) Mini Estadi

b) Ciutat Esportiva Joan Gamper

c) Camp Nou B

Correct Answer: b)

In what year did FC Barcelona sign the Argentine midfielder Javier Mascherano?

a) 2010

b) 2011

c) 2012

Correct Answer: a)

Who is the only player to have won the FIFA World Player of the Year award while representing FC Barcelona?

a) Ronaldinho

b) Lionel Messi

c) Xavi Hernandez

Correct Answer: b)

What is the name of FC Barcelona's official online store where fans can purchase club merchandise?

a) Barça Shop

b) Blaugrana Store

c) FC Barcelona Megastore

Correct Answer: c)

Which Brazilian midfielder played alongside Ronaldinho and Deco in FC Barcelona's midfield during the mid-2000s?

a) Anderson

b) Edmilson

c) Belletti

Correct Answer: b)

In what year did FC Barcelona win their first European Cup?

a) 1958

b) 1961

c) 1965

Correct Answer: b)

Who is the current president of FC Barcelona Women's team?

a) Joan Laporta

b) Carles Tusquets

c) Maria Teixidor

Correct Answer: c)

What is the name of the former FC Barcelona player who serves as the club's director of football and is responsible for managing player transfers?

a) Andoni Zubizarreta

b) Eric Abidal

c) Guillermo Amor

Correct Answer: b)

In what year did FC Barcelona win their first Copa del Rey title?

a) 1910

b) 1912

c) 1914

Correct Answer: b)

Which former FC Barcelona player and manager is known for introducing the revolutionary "tiki-taka" style of play?

a) Johan Cruyff
b) Pep Guardiola
c) Louis van Gaal

Correct Answer: b)

FUN FACTS

FC Barcelona was founded on November 29, 1899, by a group of Swiss, English, and Catalan footballers.

The club's official anthem, "Cant del Barça," was composed by Jaume Picas and Josep Maria Espinàs.

The team plays its home matches at the Camp Nou, which is one of the largest football stadiums in Europe, with a seating capacity of over 99,000.

FC Barcelona is known for its youth academy, La Masia, which has produced many legendary players, including Lionel Messi, Xavi Hernandez, and Andrés Iniesta.

Lionel Messi, often regarded as one of the greatest footballers of all time, holds numerous records for FC Barcelona, including the all-time top scorer.

In the 2008-2009 season, FC Barcelona achieved an unprecedented feat known as the "Sextuple," winning six major titles in a single season: La Liga, UEFA Champions League, Copa del Rey, Supercopa de España, FIFA Club World Cup, and UEFA Super Cup.

FC Barcelona's traditional colors, blue and red, were inspired by the colors of the flag of Catalonia.

The club's motto is "Més que un club" (More than a club), reflecting its cultural and social significance beyond football.

FC Barcelona has a historic rivalry with Real Madrid, and matches between the two teams are known as "El Clásico."

The club is owned and operated by its supporters, with over 140,000 socios (members) who have voting rights in the presidential elections.

FC Barcelona's first crest featured the letters "FCB," and it wasn't until 1910 that the iconic blue and red stripes were incorporated.

The club's nickname, "Barça," is derived from the Catalan pronunciation of "Barcelona."

FC Barcelona's women's team, known as Barcelona Femení, has been highly successful and has won numerous domestic and international titles.

The Camp Nou has a chapel, dedicated to Saint Michael, where players can attend religious services before matches.

FC Barcelona is one of the founding members of the European Club Association (ECA), representing the interests of football clubs in Europe.

The club's museum, located at Camp Nou, is one of the most visited football museums in the world.

Johan Cruyff, a legendary player and coach for FC Barcelona, introduced the concept of "total football" to the team, emphasizing fluid and interchangeable positions.

FC Barcelona has a basketball team that competes in the Liga ACB, the top professional basketball division in Spain.

The club's anthem, "Cant del Barça," is often sung by fans at matches, creating a vibrant and passionate atmosphere.

FC Barcelona has a strong commitment to social issues and philanthropy, supporting various charitable initiatives through the Barça Foundation.

The club has a tradition of unveiling new signings at Camp Nou, where thousands of fans gather to welcome the new players.

FC Barcelona's mascot is named "Berbey," and it represents a cheerful dragon, symbolizing strength and courage.

The club's longest-serving president was Josep Lluís Núñez, who held the position from 1978 to 2000.

FC Barcelona has won the FIFA Club World Cup three times (2009, 2011, and 2015).

The term "Més que un club" not only reflects the club's identity but also its involvement in political and cultural aspects, especially during challenging times in Catalonia.

The club's famous anthem, "Cant del Barça," has lyrics in both Catalan and Spanish, reflecting the diverse linguistic culture of the region.

FC Barcelona was the first club to participate in the Joan Gamper Trophy, an annual pre-season competition held at Camp Nou in honor of the club's founder.

The Barça Innovation Hub is a knowledge and innovation platform created by FC Barcelona to explore advancements in sports science, technology, and research.

FC Barcelona's women's team achieved a historic feat by winning the UEFA Women's Champions League for the first time in the 2020-2021 season.

The club's record for the most appearances is held by Xavi Hernandez, who played 767 official matches for FC Barcelona.

FC Barcelona has a tradition of producing incredible comebacks, with the term "remontada" becoming synonymous with the team's ability to overturn significant deficits.

The "L'equip petit" (The small team) philosophy, attributed to Johan Cruyff, emphasizes the importance of skill and teamwork over physical stature.

Camp Nou's press box is named after the legendary sports journalist Agustí Montal Costa, recognizing his contributions to FC Barcelona.

FC Barcelona's official mascot, "Berbey," was introduced in 1996 and is often seen engaging with fans during matches and events.

La Masia has produced not only football players but also successful coaches, including Pep Guardiola and Luis Enrique.

FC Barcelona's esports team competes in various video game tournaments, expanding the club's presence in the digital and gaming world.

The club's first official president was Walter Wild, a Swiss national who played a crucial role in the early years of FC Barcelona.

In 1957, Laszlo Kubala, a legendary forward, became the first foreign-born player to be granted Spanish citizenship while playing for FC Barcelona.

FC Barcelona's shirt sponsor, Rakuten, signed a groundbreaking deal in 2016, making it one of the most lucrative shirt sponsorship agreements in football.

The club has a dedicated space at Camp Nou called "Espai Barça," which includes the stadium renovation, the construction of a new Palau Blaugrana (indoor arena), and other facilities.

FC Barcelona holds the distinction of being the first Spanish football club to win the domestic league and cup double, achieving this feat in the 1951-1952 season.

Camp Nou has hosted numerous international matches, including the opening ceremony and matches of the 1982 FIFA World Cup held in Spain.

The "Dream Team" era, led by Johan Cruyff as a coach, witnessed FC Barcelona winning four consecutive La Liga titles from 1991 to 1994.

The club's crest underwent a redesign in 2002, introducing a more modern and stylized version of the traditional design.

FC Barcelona's women's team achieved the historic milestone of winning the treble (Primera División, Copa de la Reina, and UEFA Women's Champions League) in the 2020-2021 season.

The Joan Gamper Trophy has featured prominent international clubs as opponents, contributing to its status as a prestigious pre-season tournament.

The famous "Mes que un club" phrase was first coined by Narcís de Carreras, a former club director, highlighting the club's identity beyond football.

The Camp Nou Experience, a guided tour of the stadium and museum, attracts millions of visitors each year, offering a behind-the-scenes look at FC Barcelona's history.

FC Barcelona's official anthem was recorded by the Barcelona Municipal Band, providing a traditional and majestic sound during official ceremonies.

The club has a unique tradition of having a mosaic displayed by the fans at Camp Nou during significant matches, creating stunning visual displays.

In the 1973-1974 season, FC Barcelona featured a front line known as "The Angels of the 90 Minutes," consisting of Johan Cruyff, Johan Neeskens, and Hugo Sotil.

FC Barcelona's official magazine, Barça Magazine, provides fans with in-depth coverage of the club's activities, history, and player interviews.

The first foreign player to be signed by FC Barcelona was the Hungarian forward Ferenc Plattkó in 1932.

FC Barcelona's basketball team, known as Barça Basket, has won multiple Spanish league titles and European competitions.

The Camp Nou press room is named after the renowned journalist Antoni Bassas, acknowledging his contributions to sports journalism.

FC Barcelona has a strong presence on social media platforms, with millions of followers across Twitter, Instagram, Facebook, and YouTube.

The club's historic comeback against Paris Saint-Germain (PSG) in the 2016-2017 UEFA Champions League is often referred to as the "Remontada."

FC Barcelona holds the record for the longest unbeaten streak in La Liga, going 43 consecutive matches without a defeat during the 2016-2018 seasons.

The club's official mascot, "Berbey," was named after the Catalan word for dragon, emphasizing the mythical and powerful nature of the creature.

The Barcelona Open, an annual tennis tournament, is sponsored by FC Barcelona, showcasing the club's involvement in various sports beyond football.

FC Barcelona's women's team played its first official match in 1970, marking an early commitment to women's football.

The club has a museum dedicated to its history and achievements, featuring trophies, memorabilia, and interactive exhibits for visitors.

In 1979, the famous Dutch trio of Johan Cruyff, Johan Neeskens, and Johnny Rep reunited at FC Barcelona, adding to the club's international allure.

The club's traditional celebration for winning titles involves players donning "Catalan" hats, known as "Barretina," during victory parades.

FC Barcelona has a dedicated esports team that competes in various video game tournaments, including Pro Evolution Soccer and Rocket League.

The Camp Nou has a VIP lounge named after the legendary Johan Cruyff, recognizing his immense contributions as a player and coach.

FC Barcelona's "Blaugrana" colors are often associated with the blue and red stripes on the team's jersey, symbolizing the sky and the blood of the players.

The club has a strong commitment to environmental sustainability and has implemented various eco-friendly initiatives at Camp Nou.

FC Barcelona played a crucial role in the establishment of the European Super League, a proposed competition that aimed to bring together top European clubs.

The club's "Golden Age" in the 1940s, under coach Enrique Fernández, saw FC Barcelona dominate Spanish football, winning multiple league titles.

FC Barcelona's anthem, "Cant del Barça," has been performed by various artists, including renowned Catalan singer Lluís Llach.

The club's official TV channel, Barça TV, provides fans with exclusive content, interviews, and live coverage of matches.

FC Barcelona's official magazine, Barça Magazine, has been published since 1953, offering insights into the club's history and activities.

The Barça Innovation Hub includes a sports technology center that explores cutting-edge advancements in sports science and performance.

FC Barcelona's women's team clinched the Copa Catalunya Femenina in the 2018-2019 season, showcasing their dominance in regional competitions.

The iconic "Blaugrana" jersey design is recognized worldwide and has inspired numerous football clubs to adopt similar striped patterns.

In 1992, FC Barcelona became the first club to win both the European Cup (now UEFA Champions League) and the Copa del Rey in the same season.

Camp Nou is equipped with a state-of-the-art scoreboard, providing fans with real-time updates and statistics during matches.

The club's official crest features the Catalan flag, known as the "Senyera," paying homage to the region's cultural identity.

FC Barcelona's anthem has been played at various international events, including the opening ceremony of the 1992 Summer Olympics in Barcelona.

The "Dream Team" era, led by Johan Cruyff, popularized the use of the 3-4-3 formation, revolutionizing tactical approaches in football.

FC Barcelona's basketball team has produced legendary players like Juan Antonio San Epifanio, also known as "Epi."

The club actively supports inclusivity and diversity, with initiatives such as the Barça Foundation's programs promoting social inclusion.

FC Barcelona's handball team, known as Barça Handbol, is one of the most successful in Europe, winning numerous domestic and international titles.

The "Barça to Qatar" partnership, established in 2016, focuses on promoting football and sports development in Qatar with the support of FC Barcelona.

FC Barcelona's historic 6-2 victory over Real Madrid at the Santiago Bernabéu in 2009 is often referred to as the "Manita" (Little Hand), symbolizing the five goals scored by Barça and one hand gesture.

Camp Nou hosted the 1989 European Cup final, where AC Milan defeated Steaua Bucharest 4-0 in what became known as the "Night of Miracles."

FC Barcelona established the Johan Cruyff Foundation in honor of the legendary player and coach, focusing on promoting sports for children with disabilities.

The Camp Nou press area has a "Cruyff Zone," dedicated to Johan Cruyff's legacy and contributions to the club.

In 2017, FC Barcelona's women's team played a friendly match against the national team of Qatar, contributing to the promotion of women's football.

The club's anthem, "Cant del Barça," features lyrics that celebrate FC Barcelona's commitment to Catalan culture and its role as a symbol of unity.

FC Barcelona's basketball team achieved the rare feat of winning the EuroLeague, Liga ACB, and Copa del Rey in the 2002-2003 season.

The "Mes que un club" philosophy extends beyond football, with FC Barcelona engaging in various humanitarian projects globally.

Camp Nou's grandstand is named after Josep Suñol, a former club president who played a key role in the early development of FC Barcelona.

FC Barcelona actively promotes healthy living and sports participation through initiatives such as the "Barça Wellbeing" program.

The "Cantera Blaugrana" refers to FC Barcelona's youth academy, emphasizing the development of young talents for the first team.

FC Barcelona's women's team made history by participating in the first edition of the UEFA Women's Champions League in the 2000-2001 season.

The club's official website, Barça TV+, and mobile app provide fans with exclusive content, interviews, and live streaming.

FC Barcelona's football schools, known as "Barça Academy," operate globally, offering training programs and promoting the club's playing style.

The "Palau Blaugrana" is an indoor arena adjacent to Camp Nou, hosting various sports events, concerts, and other entertainment activities.

* * * END * * *

NOTES

www.ingramcontent.com/pod-product-compliance
Lightning Source LLC
Chambersburg PA
CBHW050727260726
48661CB00001B/110